ABRAHAM LINCOLN

BOOK FOR CURIOUS KIDS

Discover the Fascinating Life
and Legacy of America's
Beloved President

MARK LYLANI

TABLE OF CONTENTS

INTRODUCTION

Have you ever imagined what it would be like to grow up in a simple log cabin surrounded by the vast wilderness of early America? Or how someone faced with hardships and loss could rise to become the leader of a nation during its most challenging period? Join us on an exciting journey through the remarkable life of Abraham Lincoln, one of America's most beloved and respected presidents.

Abraham Lincoln's story is one of resilience, determination, and unwavering principles. Born in a humble log cabin in Kentucky, Lincoln's childhood was marked by hard work, learning, and the bonds of family. As he grew older, Lincoln faced numerous challenges and setbacks, but he never gave up on his dreams of making a difference in the world.

In this book, we will explore the incredible journey of Abraham Lincoln—from his early years in the wilderness to his presidency and the pivotal moments that defined his legacy. Along the way, we'll uncover fascinating anecdotes and personal experiences that reveal Lincoln's character and the values that guided him through life.

Get ready to discover how a young boy from a log cabin became known as "Honest Abe," the leader who united a nation torn apart by war and whose impact continues to inspire us today. Let's embark on an adventure into the life and legacy of Abraham Lincoln, a true champion of freedom and equality!

Early Years

Once upon a time, in a cozy log cabin nestled in the wilds of Kentucky, a special baby boy named Abraham Lincoln was born on February 12, 1809. His parents, Thomas and Nancy Lincoln, were hardworking pioneers with big dreams for their growing family.

Abraham, or "Abe" as everyone called him, came from a long line of brave explorers. His ancestors had traveled all the way from England to settle in America, seeking new opportunities. They journeyed through bustling cities and vast forests, finally making their home in Kentucky.

Abraham's family had a fascinating history. His grandfather, Captain Abraham Lincoln, moved the family from Virginia to Kentucky. Still, sadly, the captain lost his life in an Indian raid when Thomas, Abe's father, was just a young boy.

Thomas Lincoln had a tough upbringing, working odd jobs in Kentucky and Tennessee before settling down in Hardin County, Kentucky, where he met and married Nancy Hanks. Together, they started their own little family, with Sarah being the oldest, followed by Abe and a baby named Thomas, who didn't get to stay very long.

Life wasn't always easy for the Lincolns. Thomas worked as a farmer, cabinetmaker, and carpenter, but he faced many challenges with his land. He bought and leased farms in Kentucky but often had trouble keeping them because of disputes over property rights.

In 1816, the family decided to make a fresh start and moved to Indiana. They settled in Hurricane Township, which was like stepping into an enchanted forest. Indiana had just become a "free" state, meaning it didn't allow new enslaved people, but sadly, people who were already enslaved remained in bondage.

Young Abe loved exploring the woods and listening to the stories of settlers and Native Americans. Life in Indiana was tough, but the family worked hard and never gave up. They belonged to a church that believed in fairness and kindness, and they made sure to follow the rules against dancing, drinking alcohol, and slavery.

Despite their challenges, Thomas Lincoln finally managed to secure 80 acres of land in Indiana in 1827. This was a big relief for the family and gave them hope for a brighter future.

Little Abe grew up surrounded by nature, learning to read and write from his mother and dreaming of making a difference in the world. His adventures in the Indiana wilderness shaped him into the courageous and compassionate leader he would later become.

Challenges and Changes

Life took a tragic turn for young Abraham Lincoln when his family faced a devastating loss. On October 5, 1818, at just nine years old, Abraham experienced the death of his beloved mother, Nancy Lincoln, from a sickness known as milk sickness. This illness was caused by consuming milk or meat from cows that had grazed on white snakeroot plants containing a toxic compound called tremetol. In frontier areas like Indiana, where the Lincolns lived, such illnesses were unfortunately common due to the free-ranging nature of cattle.

Nancy's passing left a significant responsibility on Abraham's older sister,

Sarah, who now had to take charge of their household along with their father and cousin, Dennis Hanks.

Abraham was a thoughtful and curious boy who loved to read and learn, but he found the hard work of farm life to be tough. His father, Thomas Lincoln, thought Abraham was lazy because he preferred books and writing over physical labor.

On December 2, 1819, Thomas Lincoln married Sarah Bush Johnston, a widow with three children. Abraham quickly grew fond of his new stepmother and began calling her "Mother." She understood that Abraham didn't enjoy farm work but admired his love for reading and encouraged his intellectual pursuits.

Ten years after Nancy's passing, tragedy struck again when Abraham's sister Sarah passed away while giving birth to a stillborn baby. This loss deeply affected Abraham, leaving him heartbroken and in mourning.

Despite the challenges and losses he faced, Abraham Lincoln's determination to learn and grow never wavered. With the support and love of his stepmother, he found solace in books and continued to nurture his passion for knowledge, paving the way for his extraordinary journey ahead.

A Journey of Discovery

Abraham Lincoln's early education was unlike that of most children. Born in a log cabin on the frontier, Lincoln's schooling was limited, but his thirst for knowledge was boundless.

Lincoln's formal education was brief and sporadic. He learned to read from itinerant teachers who traveled through his rural community. In Kentucky and later in Indiana, where his family moved, Lincoln's school attendance was interrupted by farm chores, allowing him fewer than 12 months of schooling by the time he was 15 years old. Despite this, Lincoln remained a passionate reader throughout his life.

At an early age, Lincoln discovered a love for books. He devoured the pages of the King James Bible, Aesop's Fables, John Bunyan's The Pilgrim's Progress, Daniel Defoe's Robinson Crusoe, and Benjamin Franklin's Autobiography. These stories not only entertained him but also sparked his curiosity about the world beyond his frontier home.

Lincoln's father, Thomas, increasingly relied on him for farm work and hired him out to earn extra money for the family. Lincoln's physical strength and skill with an axe made him an indispensable worker. He even became a county wrestling champion, known for his athleticism and audacity.

In 1830, Lincoln's family moved to Illinois to escape the threat of milk sickness. Abraham, now a young man, began to feel distant from his father, who did not share his passion for education. When the family prepared to move again in 1831, Abraham decided to strike out on his own.

Settling in New Salem, Illinois, Abraham Lincoln embarked on a new chapter of his life. Here, he continued his self-education while working odd jobs and exploring new opportunities. He even embarked on a journey to New Orleans, Louisiana, where he witnessed the harsh realities of slavery for the first time.

Love and Loss

In the small town of New Salem, Abraham Lincoln's life took a momentous turn when he met Mary Todd, a spirited and intelligent woman from a wealthy Kentucky family. They crossed paths in 1839, and their connection blossomed quickly. Despite a brief pause in their engagement, Lincoln and Mary were married in 1842.

Mary Todd brought vitality and charm to Lincoln's life. She was known for her strong personality and keen intellect, which complemented Lincoln's more reserved demeanor. Together, they embarked on a life filled with promise and challenges.

The Lincoln household became a bustling center of family life. Their eldest son, Robert Todd Lincoln, was born in 1843, marking the beginning of their family journey. However, their happiness was tempered by tragedy when their second son, Edward (known as Eddie), passed away at a young age. Despite this heartbreaking loss, the family found solace and joy in the birth of their other children.

Their third son, Willie, brought them much happiness but faced illness during Lincoln's lifetime. The youngest, Thomas (nicknamed Tad), was a source of boundless energy and laughter, though he also encountered health challenges later in life.

Abraham Lincoln deeply cherished his children and was known for his kindness towards them. Despite his busy work life, Lincoln was a loving father who cared deeply for his family. The losses of Eddie and Willie were especially difficult for Lincoln and his wife, Mary. Lincoln struggled with periods of profound sadness, and Mary faced her own challenges in coping with these heartbreaking losses.

Exploring Opportunities

In the early 1830s, Abraham Lincoln found himself in New Salem, Illinois, where he embarked on new and exciting endeavors. He began working at a general store, learning the ins and outs of business and serving the townspeople.

In 1832, Abraham Lincoln decided to run for a position in the Illinois House of Representatives. However, his plans took an unexpected turn when he joined the Illinois Militia to serve in the Black Hawk War.

The Black Hawk War was a conflict that occurred in 1832 between the United States and Native American tribes, primarily led by Chief Black Hawk of the Sauk tribe. Black Hawk and his followers resisted the forced removal of their people from their ancestral lands in Illinois, which had been promised to them in previous treaties.

Abraham Lincoln enlisted in the Illinois Militia and was elected as a captain during this conflict. Although the war was relatively brief and ended with the defeat of Black Hawk's forces, it provided Lincoln with valuable experiences and lessons in leadership. Serving in the militia gave him firsthand insights into military life, strategic decision-making, and the challenges of leading men in battle.

After returning from the war, Lincoln considered becoming a blacksmith but instead teamed up with a young man named William Berry to buy a general store. To sell beverages at the store, Lincoln and Berry obtained bartending licenses and turned their business into a tavern. They sold spirits and food, attracting customers from near and far. Despite the booming economy, their partnership faced challenges when Berry struggled with alcoholism, leaving Lincoln to manage the store on his own.

During this time, Lincoln entered politics and ran for a seat in the state legislature. He spoke passionately about the need for improvements along the Sangamon River, drawing crowds with his storytelling skills. Despite his efforts, Lincoln faced tough competition and did not win the election, but he gained valuable experience and learned important lessons.

Lincoln also took on roles as New Salem's postmaster and later as a county surveyor. Throughout these busy years, Lincoln continued to read voraciously and developed a strong interest in the law. Instead of studying with an established attorney, Lincoln borrowed legal books and taught himself law, determined to pursue a career as a lawyer.

Path to Leadership

Abraham Lincoln's journey into politics and law began with his deep commitment to his community and a passion for standing up for important causes. In 1834, Lincoln ran for the Illinois State House of Representatives as a member of the Whig Party, winning against a powerful opponent. This victory marked the start of his four terms in the Illinois House, representing Sangamon County.

During his time in the state legislature, Lincoln advocated for the construction of the Illinois and Michigan Canal, which would improve transportation and boost economic growth in the region. He also supported expanding suffrage to all white males, believing in the importance of democratic participation.

Lincoln's views on slavery evolved over time. While he opposed the institution of slavery and believed it was unjust, he also opposed immediate abolition, fearing that it could lead to greater conflicts and hardships. Instead, Lincoln supported gradual emancipation and colonization efforts, inspired by Henry Clay's ideas.

Henry Clay, a prominent statesman and senator known as the "Great Compromiser," proposed a plan known as the American Colonization Society. This plan advocated for the gradual emancipation of enslaved people and their resettlement in Africa or the Caribbean. Clay's approach resonated with Lincoln, who believed in the importance of finding a practical solution to the complex issue of slavery. Lincoln admired Clay's efforts to seek compromise and unity, even in the face of deeply entrenched divisions over slavery.

In 1836, Lincoln achieved a significant milestone by becoming a licensed attorney in Illinois. He moved to Springfield to practice law under John T. Stuart, who was also Mary Todd's cousin. Lincoln quickly gained a reputation as a skilled trial lawyer, known for his sharp cross-examinations and persuasive closing arguments.

One of Lincoln's most poignant speeches occurred in 1838 at the Springfield Lyceum following the tragic murder of Elijah Parish Lovejoy. Lovejoy, an outspoken abolitionist, and journalist, courageously used his newspaper, the "Alton Observer," to denounce slavery and advocate for the rights of African Americans. His steadfast dedication to these ideals made him a target of hostility from pro-slavery factions in Illinois.

In November 1837, Lovejoy's printing press was destroyed by a mob in Alton, Illinois, seeking to silence his abolitionist message. Undeterred, Lovejoy continued to publish his anti-slavery newspaper. However, tensions escalated, and on November 7, 1837, Lovejoy was fatally shot while defending his printing press from another attack by a pro-slavery mob.

In this speech, Lincoln emphasized the importance of preserving the United States as a nation and warned against internal threats to its stability.

The events of Lincoln's early career, coupled with his unwavering commitment to serving his community and advocating for justice, laid the groundwork for his future leadership and shaped his perspectives on equality and the role of government.

Embracing Whig Principles

Abraham Lincoln believed in the Whig Party, a group that stood for certain ideas and goals. The Whigs wanted to make America stronger and more modern. They thought the government should help businesses grow and build things like roads and railroads to connect different parts of the country. They also wanted to protect American industries from foreign competition by placing taxes on goods brought in from other countries.

The Whigs believed in a strong federal government that could bring the states together and solve big problems. They didn't like it when the president had too much power, especially Andrew Jackson, who they thought was too focused on himself. The Whigs wanted a balance of power between different parts of the government.

In 1843, Abraham Lincoln tried to become a member of Congress as a Whig, but he didn't win. He didn't give up, though. Three years later, in 1846, Lincoln tried again, and this time, he succeeded. He became the only Whig in the Illinois delegation to Congress.

As a Whig congressman, Lincoln worked hard on committees that dealt with things like how the post office operated and how money was spent on the military. He wanted to make sure the government used money wisely and helped people in need.

One important thing Lincoln did in Congress was team up with another congressman named Joshua R. Giddings. They worked on a law to end slavery in Washington, D.C., the capital of the United States. They thought it was unfair and wanted to find a way to stop it gradually by paying enslavers for their slaves.

Abraham Lincoln's time as a Whig congressman showed his dedication to making America better by following the Whig principles of economic growth, national unity, and fair government.

Standing Up for His Beliefs

Abraham Lincoln didn't always agree with everything the government did. When the United States went to war with Mexico in 1846, Lincoln spoke out against it. The war was sparked by a border dispute between the United States and Mexico over Texas. President James K. Polk, seeking to expand U.S. territory, used this dispute as a pretext to instigate war.

Lincoln believed that President Polk's motives were driven by a desire for "military glory," which he felt came at the cost of many lives. This war ultimately resulted in significant territorial gains for the United

States through the Treaty of Guadalupe Hidalgo in 1848. Still, it was a controversial conflict that faced opposition from individuals like Lincoln, who questioned its motives and consequences.

One important issue for Lincoln was the Wilmot Proviso. This was a proposal to stop slavery in any new territories that the United States gained from Mexico. Lincoln supported this idea because he didn't want slavery to spread into new lands.

To show how much he disagreed with President Polk, Lincoln came up with something called the Spot Resolutions. He wanted Polk to show exactly where American blood had been shed on American soil during the war with Mexico. Lincoln believed that the war wasn't necessary and that the president was misleading the country.

Unfortunately, not everyone agreed with Lincoln. Congress ignored his resolutions, and newspapers made fun of him, giving him the nickname "spotty Lincoln." This made it hard for him to get support from people in his home district.

In 1846, Lincoln promised to serve only one term in Congress. When it was time for a new president to be chosen in 1848, Lincoln supported General Zachary Taylor as the nominee for the Whig Party. Taylor won the election, but Lincoln didn't get the job he hoped for in Taylor's administration. Instead, he returned to his law practice in Illinois.

Abraham Lincoln's actions during this time showed that he wasn't afraid to stand up for what he believed was right, even if it meant going against powerful people like the president. He continued to work hard as a lawyer and kept thinking about ways to make the country better for everyone.

The Lawyer

Abraham Lincoln was not just a politician; he was also a hardworking lawyer in Springfield, Illinois. He took on all kinds of cases that came before him, from property disputes to criminal trials. Twice a year, for ten weeks at a time, Lincoln traveled to different county courts across the state to represent his clients. He did this for 16 years!

One of Lincoln's big areas of legal work involved transportation cases during a time when the country was expanding westward. He often dealt with disputes between riverboat operators and the new railroad companies, especially when river barges had trouble passing under the new railroad bridges. At first, Lincoln favored the riverboat interests because he used to work on riverboats himself, but later on, he represented anyone who needed his help.

In a famous case known as Hurd v. Rock Island Bridge Company, Abraham Lincoln played a pivotal role as lead counsel for the railroad company in a significant legal battle. This case emerged against the backdrop of America's westward expansion, which Lincoln strongly supported.

The conflict arose in 1856 when a steamboat collided with the newly constructed Rock Island bridge spanning the Mississippi River between Rock Island, Illinois, and Davenport, Iowa—a historic milestone as the first railroad bridge to cross the mighty river.

The steamboat's owner, Captain John Hurd, sought damages and claimed that the bridge posed a hazard to navigation, leading to a lawsuit filed in the U.S. Circuit Court in Chicago. Lincoln's legal skills were put to the test as he defended the interests of the Rock Island Railroad before a jury trial presided over by Supreme Court Justice John McLean.

During the trial, Lincoln adeptly presented arguments in favor of the railroad's right to construct the bridge, addressing complex legal issues surrounding navigation rights and interstate commerce. The jury's deadlock at 9 to 3 in favor of the railroad was seen as a surprising victory, underscoring Lincoln's prowess as a trial attorney.

Lincoln's legal career was impressive. He appeared before the Illinois Supreme Court in 175 cases, winning most of them. One of his biggest clients was the Illinois Central Railroad. His honesty and integrity earned him the nickname "Honest Abe" among his colleagues and clients.

One of Lincoln's most famous courtroom moments came during a criminal trial in 1858. He defended a man named William "Duff" Armstrong, who was accused of murder. Lincoln used a Farmers' Almanac to challenge an eyewitness's testimony about seeing the crime in the moonlight. His clever tactics helped win the case, and Armstrong was acquitted.

As Lincoln's reputation grew, he took on even more high-profile cases. In 1859, he defended Simeon Quinn "Peachy" Harrison, a relative of his political opponent, in a murder trial. Lincoln's passionate defense and legal skills led to Harrison's acquittal.

44

The Inventor

Abraham Lincoln once had an idea that would help boats glide over shoals and river obstacles more easily. This idea came from his experiences traveling on rivers where boats often got stuck in shallow areas.

When Lincoln was young, he worked on flatboats that traveled down rivers like the Ohio and Mississippi. One time, the boat he was on got stuck on a milldam near Springfield, Illinois. Lincoln took charge of the situation by unloading cargo and even drilling a hole in the boat to drain water and make it lighter. With some help, he managed to get the boat over the obstruction.

Inspired by these challenges, Lincoln came up with an invention. He designed a system of inflatable bellows that could be attached to the sides of a boat. These bellows, like large air chambers, could be filled with air to lift the boat over shallow areas or obstacles in the water.

In 1849, Lincoln filed a patent application for his invention. The United States Patent Office granted him Patent No. 6,469 on May 22 of that year. Although Lincoln's invention was never put into practical use, it showcased his ingenuity and problem-solving skills.

Today, Lincoln's patent model is on display at the Smithsonian Institution. This model reminds us that Abraham Lincoln was not only a great president but also a curious thinker and inventor who wanted to find solutions to real-world challenges.

Standing Against Slavery

In the mid-1800s, America was deeply divided over the issue of slavery. The North, where Abraham Lincoln lived, opposed slavery, while the South supported it. This tension only grew worse when the Compromise of 1850 failed to settle the slavery debate.

Abraham Lincoln greatly admired Henry Clay, a leader who believed in ending slavery gradually. However, as tensions rose, Illinois Senator Stephen A. Douglas proposed a compromise called popular sovereignty. This plan let each territory decide for itself whether to allow slavery.

Many Northerners, including Lincoln, were worried. They feared that popular sovereignty could spread slavery into new territories. In 1854, Congress passed the Kansas-Nebraska Act, which allowed territories like Kansas and Nebraska to decide their slavery status. This made Lincoln upset.

In a powerful speech called the "Peoria Speech," Lincoln openly opposed slavery. He hated slavery because he believed it was unjust and hurt America's reputation as a land of freedom.

In 1854, Lincoln was elected to the Illinois legislature but chose not to take his seat. Instead, he set his sights on the United States Senate. Even though he led in the early rounds of voting, he eventually withdrew to support Lyman Trumbull, an anti-slavery Democrat.

Abraham Lincoln's stand against slavery marked his return to politics. He was determined to keep America united and free from the evils of slavery, setting the stage for his future leadership in a divided nation.

MARK LYLANI

Responding to the Dred Scott Decision

In the mid-1800s, America was deeply divided over the issue of slavery. Tensions escalated with a pivotal moment in 1857 when the Supreme Court issued a landmark ruling in the Dred Scott v. Sandford case. This decision had a profound impact on the nation's future and ignited strong responses from figures like Abraham Lincoln.

The Dred Scott case revolved around Dred Scott, an enslaved African American man who had lived in free states and territories where slavery was prohibited. Scott sued for his freedom, arguing that his time in free areas made him legally free. However, the Supreme Court's decision shocked many by ruling that African Americans, whether enslaved or free, were not and could never become citizens of the United States. The court also declared that Congress had no power to ban slavery in the territories, effectively allowing the expansion of slavery into new regions.

Abraham Lincoln, a rising political figure at the time, strongly opposed the Dred Scott decision. He believed it was unjust and threatened the core principles of equality and freedom. Lincoln argued that the Founding Fathers had intended to limit the spread of slavery and that the Supreme Court had overstepped its authority.

In response to the Dred Scott decision, Lincoln delivered powerful speeches and engaged in debates to challenge its legality and moral implications. He saw the decision as part of a broader effort by pro-slavery forces to extend slavery's reach across the nation, leading him to redouble his efforts to resist this expansion.

Through his unwavering opposition to the Dred Scott decision, Lincoln aimed to unite Americans who opposed slavery and defend the principles of freedom and equality.

The Birth of a New Party

In the mid-1800s, the United States was undergoing profound changes, especially when it came to the issue of slavery. As tensions mounted and the Whig Party found itself increasingly divided over this contentious issue, a new political force emerged: the Republican Party.

Abraham Lincoln, a rising figure in Illinois politics, played a pivotal role in this transition. The Whig Party, once a prominent political force, began to fracture over its stance on slavery. Some Whigs, like Lincoln, were deeply opposed to the expansion of slavery into new territories. This stance put them at odds with other Whigs who were more willing to compromise on the issue.

As the Whig Party disintegrated, Lincoln and other anti-slavery activists saw an opportunity to form a new political party that would oppose the spread of slavery and advocate for free labor. In 1854, the Republican Party was officially founded, bringing together former Whigs, anti-slavery Democrats, and members of other smaller parties who shared a commitment to halting the expansion of slavery.

Abraham Lincoln quickly aligned himself with the new Republican Party and became one of its leading figures in Illinois. His eloquent speeches and persuasive arguments against the immorality of slavery resonated with many Americans, especially in the North. Lincoln's leadership and dedication to the anti-slavery cause helped propel him onto the national stage.

The Republican Party's platform centered on opposition to the Kansas-Nebraska Act, which allowed new territories to decide for themselves whether to permit slavery—a measure that was seen as a capitulation to pro-slavery forces. This act, coupled with the Supreme Court's infamous Dred Scott decision in 1857, further inflamed anti-slavery sentiment in the North and galvanized support for the Republicans.

Abraham Lincoln's role in the formation and rise of the Republican Party marked a turning point in American politics. His steadfast commitment to opposing the spread of slavery, combined with his political acumen and moral clarity, helped reshape the national debate and ultimately led to his election as the 16th President of the United States in 1860.

As the country hurtled toward civil war, the Republican Party under Lincoln's leadership would confront the existential crisis of slavery head-on, setting the stage for one of the most transformative periods in American history.

A Nation in Conflict

In the years leading up to 1856, the nation was deeply divided over the issue of slavery. Abraham Lincoln, although not yet president, played a significant role in these turbulent times.

As the 1856 elections approached, Lincoln joined the newly formed Republican Party in Illinois. This party opposed the spread of slavery into new territories and supported the admission of Kansas as a free state. Lincoln attended the Bloomington Convention, where he delivered a powerful speech in support of the party's platform and emphasized the importance of preserving the Union.

During the Republican National Convention in June 1856, Lincoln received support to run as vice president, but the ticket was ultimately led by John C. Frémont and William Dayton. Despite this, Lincoln wholeheartedly supported the Republican candidates throughout Illinois.

Meanwhile, the Democrats nominated James Buchanan for president, and the Know-Nothings (officially known as the Native American Party before 1855 and later as the American Party) nominated Millard Fillmore.

The Know Nothings party was a nativist political movement in the United States in the 1850s. Its members were required to say "I know nothing" when outsiders asked about its specifics, which gave the group its colloquial name.

Buchanan won the election, but Lincoln's influence within the Republican Party continued to grow, especially in Illinois.

The Dred Scott v. Sandford case in 1857 further inflamed tensions over slavery. Dred Scott was an enslaved person who had been taken by his master to a free territory, where he sought his freedom through the courts. However, the Supreme Court, under Chief Justice Roger B. Taney, ruled against Scott, declaring that black people were not citizens and had no rights under the Constitution. This decision also declared the Missouri Compromise unconstitutional, allowing slavery to potentially expand into new territories.

Lincoln strongly condemned the Dred Scott decision, accusing Democrats of conspiring to support the "Slave Power." He argued that the decision contradicted the principles of the Declaration of Independence, which declared that all men were entitled to certain inalienable rights, including life, liberty, and the pursuit of happiness.

These events marked a critical turning point in American politics, setting the stage for further debates and conflicts over the future of slavery in the United States.

The Great Senate Campaign

In 1858, Abraham Lincoln wanted to become a U.S. Senator, and he faced a tough opponent named Stephen Douglas. Many people believed that Lincoln, a former Whig, should be the candidate for the Illinois Republicans. After campaigning and supporting Lyman Trumbull in 1856, Lincoln earned the nomination with little opposition at the first-ever Illinois Republican convention.

Lincoln was excited to accept the nomination and gave a famous speech called the "House Divided" speech. He talked about how a nation couldn't survive if it was divided over the issue of slavery. Lincoln believed that the United States needed to choose to be either all free or all slave, or else it could face serious problems.

The big showdown came during seven debates between Lincoln and Douglas across Illinois. These debates were like big contests, drawing huge crowds and national attention. Lincoln warned about the dangers of slavery and accused Douglas of not valuing equality like the Founding Fathers did.

Douglas believed in letting local settlers decide about slavery, even though the Dred Scott decision said otherwise. Lincoln argued that Douglas was promoting slavery and going against what was right.

Even though the Democrats won more seats in the legislature, Lincoln's powerful arguments made people notice him all across the country. He even bought a German-language newspaper to get more Republican support.

After the election in 1858, Lincoln's name started popping up as a possible presidential candidate, but he wasn't sure if he wanted to run for president. Still, he kept working hard, making speeches all over. He was popular in the Midwest but not as much in the East.

In February 1860, Lincoln was invited to speak at Cooper Union in New York. This was a big deal because it showcased his smart ideas. He argued against popular sovereignty and said slavery was wrong. Even though some people thought he looked funny, Lincoln's speech impressed many people and made them think he could be a good leader.

Lincoln's journey toward becoming president was filled with hard work and smart moves. He became a leader of the Republican Party, getting more and more support as people saw him as a possible president.

The Path to Victory

In May 1860, Abraham Lincoln's supporters gathered at the Illinois Republican State Convention in Decatur. They formed a campaign team led by David Davis, Norman Judd, Leonard Swett, and Jesse DuBois to help Lincoln secure his first endorsement. They highlighted Lincoln's background as a rail splitter, which earned him the nickname "The Rail Candidate."

A few weeks later, on May 18, at the Republican National Convention in Chicago, Lincoln won the nomination on the third ballot. He beat out other candidates like

Seward and Chase. Hannibal Hamlin of Maine, a former Democrat, was chosen as Lincoln's running mate to balance the ticket.

Lincoln's nomination was a result of his moderate views on slavery, his support for internal improvements, and his stance on tariffs that reassured Pennsylvania's iron interests.

During the campaign, the country was deeply divided over the issue of slavery. Lincoln's election was seen as a turning point by many Republicans who believed that the North had been treated unfairly by the Southern states. Despite fears of secession (states leaving the Union), Lincoln's supporters were confident that his election would not lead to war.

The Northern Democrats nominated Stephen Douglas, while Southern Democrats chose John C. Breckinridge. Another party, the Constitutional Union Party, nominated John Bell. Lincoln mainly focused on campaigning in the North, relying on strong Republican support.

To rally voters, the Lincoln campaign created a youth organization called the Wide Awakes. They helped with voter registration drives and organized rallies to support Lincoln. The campaign highlighted Lincoln's humble beginnings and his rise to prominence through hard work.

Finally, on November 6, 1860, Abraham Lincoln made history by becoming the 16th president of the United States. He won the election without receiving any votes from most Southern states. Instead, he secured decisive victories in the North and West.

Lincoln's election marked a challenging time for the nation as it faced divisions over slavery. This outcome hinted at the tough road ahead as the country headed into a difficult and divisive period in its history.

Heading to the White House

In 1860, Abraham Lincoln won a historic election to become the 16th President of the United States. However, his victory stirred deep concerns in the Southern states. Many feared that Lincoln would try to change their way of life, especially regarding slavery.

As Lincoln prepared to take office in early 1861, several Southern states decided to leave the Union. They believed that Lincoln's presidency threatened their rights and traditions. South Carolina led the way by officially seceding on December 20, 1860, followed by other states like Mississippi,

Florida, Alabama, Georgia, Louisiana, and Texas.

Lincoln was determined to preserve the Union. Despite the growing crisis, he reassured everyone that he had no plans to interfere with slavery where it already existed. His inauguration on March 4, 1861, was met with tension and worry. To reach Washington, D.C., safely, Lincoln traveled in disguise and under heavy guard due to threats against him.

In his inaugural speech, Lincoln appealed to the Southern states to remain united with the North. He emphasized that the main cause of the crisis was the disagreement over slavery—whether it should expand into new territories or not.

Despite Lincoln's efforts to keep the peace, the country was moving toward a conflict. Both sides were deeply committed to their beliefs, and Lincoln faced the daunting task of leading the nation through these turbulent times.

The Beginning of the Civil War

When Abraham Lincoln became president in 1861, tensions between the North and South were very high. Union soldiers were stationed at Fort Sumter in Charleston, South Carolina. The person in charge there, Major Robert Anderson, asked for more supplies from Washington.

Lincoln agreed to send supplies to Fort Sumter. However, this decision upset people in the Southern states who wanted to leave the United States and were called secessionists. They saw this act as a declaration of war.

On April 12, 1861, Confederate forces (those who wanted to break away from the United States) fired at Fort Sumter. This event marked the beginning of the Civil War.

Before this happened, Lincoln hoped to avoid a war. He didn't realize how serious the situation was. He thought the Southern states wouldn't actually leave the Union. The attack on Fort Sumter surprised him.

After the attack, Lincoln asked the states to send 75,000 volunteer soldiers to protect Washington, recapture forts, and keep the country together. This request made states pick sides. Some states, like Virginia, North Carolina, Tennessee, and Arkansas, decided to join the Confederacy (the Southern states that left the Union). Others, like Maryland, tried to stay neutral.

When Union troops moved through Baltimore, they faced angry mobs who tried to stop them. To protect the soldiers, Lincoln suspended something called "habeas corpus," which is a legal rule that protects people from being arrested unlawfully. This caused a disagreement with Chief Justice Roger B. Taney, who believed only Congress could suspend this rule.

The attack on Fort Sumter made people in the North want to defend their country, while those in the South were determined to break away. Lincoln had a big challenge: to keep the United States together and deal with the growing split between the North and South as the Civil War began.

Leading the Union

Abraham Lincoln faced a big challenge when some Southern states decided to leave the United States and create their own country, called the Confederate States of America. As president, Lincoln had to make important decisions to keep the nation together.

Lincoln took charge of the Union's military plans to stop the Confederates. He did things that had never been done before, like blocking Confederate ports and arresting people suspected of helping the South. Even though some people disagreed with him, most of Congress and the northern states supported his actions.

Lincoln had to manage disagreements within his own party. Some wanted him to end slavery right away, while others thought he was moving too slowly. In 1861, he signed a law that allowed the Union to take away and free slaves who were helping the Confederates.

When one of his generals tried to free rebel enslaved people without permission, Lincoln stopped him. He believed that such decisions should be carefully planned to avoid causing more problems.

Internationally, Lincoln worked hard to prevent other countries from helping the Confederates. He also had to deal with a tense situation called the Trent Affair, in which the U.S. Navy stopped a British ship carrying Confederate diplomats. Lincoln defused the situation by letting them go.

Lincoln kept a close eye on the war efforts and talked with governors and generals regularly. He even hired a new Secretary of War, Edwin Stanton, to make things run more smoothly and stop people from cheating the government.

Lincoln's plan focused on protecting Washington, D.C., and winning the war quickly. He learned a lot about military tactics and understood how important certain places, like the Mississippi River, were to winning the war.

Throughout the war, Lincoln listened to experienced military leaders and even visited West Point for advice. By making careful decisions and working with his team, Lincoln led the Union through tough times and worked hard to keep the country united.

Challenges in Command

After a tough defeat at Bull Run and the retirement of General Winfield Scott, President Lincoln chose General George B. McClellan to lead the Union forces. McClellan spent a long time planning his attack in Virginia, which made Lincoln impatient. McClellan thought there were enough troops to protect Washington, but Lincoln disagreed.

In 1862, Lincoln replaced McClellan because he wasn't taking enough action. He put General Henry Halleck in charge and appointed General John Pope to lead a new army. Lincoln hoped Pope could attack

Richmond from the north to protect Washington, but Pope was defeated at the Second Battle of Bull Run.

Even though Lincoln wasn't happy with McClellan, he put him back in charge near Washington. Soon after, General Robert E. Lee's Confederate forces entered Maryland, leading to the Battle of Antietam, which was a big Union win. This battle allowed Lincoln to issue the Emancipation Proclamation in January 1863.

McClellan didn't do what Lincoln wanted after Antietam, so Lincoln replaced him with General Ambrose Burnside. Burnside launched an attack at Fredericksburg, but it ended in defeat. Lincoln then chose General Joseph Hooker, but Lee also defeated Hooker at Chancellorsville.

Despite these setbacks, General George Meade won a crucial victory at Gettysburg, but he didn't follow up as Lincoln had hoped. Meanwhile, General Ulysses S. Grant was making progress in the West, capturing Vicksburg and gaining control of the Mississippi River.

The year 1863 was tough for Lincoln's generals, with victories and defeats, but Lincoln kept pushing forward, looking for ways to end the war and bring the country back together. He knew that choosing the right leaders and making tough decisions were important steps toward victory.

MARK LYLANI

The Fight for Freedom

Before 1865, the United States Constitution didn't let the federal government end slavery, leaving it up to individual states. President Lincoln thought that stopping slavery from spreading into new places would make it go away over time. He hoped that by letting new states be free, they would eventually be more than the states where slavery was allowed.

Lincoln wanted to convince states to agree to pay enslavers to let their slaves go free. But he said no to Major Generals John C. Frémont and David Hunter when they tried to set slaves free with military orders because he was worried it might make border states that were staying loyal want to leave.

In June 1862, Congress passed a law that said there couldn't be slavery in federal areas, which Lincoln liked. The Confiscation Act of 1862 let enslaved people go free if they belonged to people helping the rebellion, even though Lincoln wasn't sure if it was okay under the Constitution.

On July 22, 1862, Lincoln talked about the Emancipation Proclamation with his cabinet. Even though Peace Democrats (Copperheads) who didn't want to free slaves were pushing against it, Lincoln decided to support it after talking with Republican editor Horace Greeley.

Lincoln wrote a letter to Greeley saying that his main goal was to save the country. He said he'd free all the slaves, some of them, or none at all, if it would help keep the country together.

On September 22, 1862, Lincoln issued the first Emancipation Proclamation, declaring that slaves in states fighting against the Union would be free on January 1, 1863. For the next 100 days, Lincoln prepared the country and the military for this big change.

Even though Lincoln tried to end the war without freeing slaves, he signed the Emancipation Proclamation on January 1, 1863. This important paper freed slaves in states that were against the Union and let Black men join the Union army.

Lincoln thought that having Black soldiers would help stop the rebellion. He asked General Andrew Johnson to get Black soldiers in Tennessee, thinking their help would make the war end faster.

By the end of 1863, because of Lincoln's leadership, thousands of African Americans had joined Union groups, which helped a lot in ending slavery and saving the country.

Leadership in Civil War Battles

During the Civil War, President Abraham Lincoln played a critical role in guiding the Union forces to victory against the Confederate states. Lincoln made important decisions that shaped the outcome of key battles, ultimately leading to the preservation of the Union and the end of slavery.

One of the most famous battles of the Civil War was the Battle of Gettysburg, which occurred from July 1 to July 3, 1863. President Lincoln closely monitored this battle and provided support to General George Meade, the Union commander.

Despite the challenging circumstances, Lincoln's leadership helped inspire Union troops to defend their positions, leading to a decisive victory that boosted morale and turned the tide of the war in favor of the Union.

Another crucial battle influenced by Lincoln's leadership was the Battle of Antietam on September 17, 1862. This battle was significant because it gave Lincoln the opportunity to issue the Emancipation Proclamation shortly afterward. By declaring that all slaves in Confederate-held territories would be free, Lincoln changed the course of the war and advanced the cause of freedom.

Lincoln's role in appointing and managing generals was also vital to the Union's success. He chose leaders like General Ulysses S. Grant, who demonstrated bold and effective strategies in battles such as Vicksburg, where the Union gained control of the Mississippi River. Lincoln's support for Grant's aggressive tactics helped pave the way for key victories that weakened the Confederacy.

Throughout the war, Lincoln's unwavering commitment to the Union and the principles of freedom guided his decisions. He understood the importance of perseverance and unity in achieving victory. Lincoln's leadership during the Civil War not only preserved the Union but also laid the foundation for a more just and united nation.

Abraham Lincoln's contributions to the Civil War were instrumental in shaping the conflict's outcome and advancing the cause of freedom for all Americans. His determination and vision continue to inspire us today as we strive to uphold the values of liberty and equality.

The Gettysburg Address

In the heart of Pennsylvania, on a crisp November afternoon in 1863, President Abraham Lincoln stood before a crowd gathered at the Soldiers' National Cemetery in Gettysburg. This was a solemn place where brave soldiers from both the Union and Confederate armies had fought and died just a few months earlier in the Battle of Gettysburg, one of the bloodiest clashes of the Civil War.

Lincoln wasn't the main speaker that day. He was invited to say a few words after the main oration. As he rose to speak, no one could have guessed that his short speech would become one of the most famous in American history.

Lincoln began with a phrase that echoed across the ages: "Four score and seven years ago." With these words, he referred to the signing of the Declaration of Independence, which had happened 87 years before. Lincoln reminded the nation that America was founded on the principle of liberty and the belief that all people are created equal.

Lincoln said the Civil War was a test for the United States. Could a nation dedicated to freedom and equality endure? He honored the soldiers who had given their lives at Gettysburg, saying it was up to the living to ensure "that these dead shall not have died in vain."

Lincoln spoke of a "new birth of freedom" that the nation must strive for—a renewed commitment to government "of the people, by the people, for the people." These words captured the essence of what America stood for: a nation where the power and authority came from its citizens.

Despite its importance, the exact words of Lincoln's speech are still debated today. There are different versions written by Lincoln himself, and contemporary newspaper accounts vary in their reporting of his speech. The exact location of where Lincoln stood to deliver the address is also a subject of historical investigation.

Before arriving in Gettysburg, Lincoln had been feeling unwell. He mentioned to his secretary that he felt dizzy and weak. After delivering the speech, Lincoln became even more ill with a fever and a severe headache.

It turned out he was suffering from a mild case of smallpox.

Lincoln's Gettysburg Address remains a powerful reminder of the sacrifices made during the Civil War and a call to preserve the ideals of freedom and equality for future generations. It's a testament to the enduring power of words and the impact they can have on history.

Uniting a Nation in Turmoil

In 1864, Abraham Lincoln faced a tough challenge: he wanted to be re-elected as President of the United States. The country was still in the middle of a war, and many people were worried about the future. But Lincoln knew that he needed to keep leading the nation to victory and to bring everyone together.

To win the election, Lincoln worked hard to bring different groups of people together. He talked to Republicans and War Democrats like Edwin M. Stanton and Andrew Johnson. He used his power to appoint people to important positions, which helped him gain support from different sides.

During the Republican convention, Lincoln's party chose Andrew Johnson as his running mate. They even created a new political party called the Union Party to show that they were bringing together all who wanted to support the country during the war.

The war wasn't going well for the Union Army, and many people were worried that Lincoln might not win the election. However, Lincoln made a secret promise: he wrote a letter saying that if he lost the election, he would still work hard to defeat the Confederacy before leaving office. He didn't show this letter to his cabinet but asked them to sign it in a sealed envelope.

The other side, the Democrats, had different opinions about the war. Their candidate, George McClellan, supported the war effort even though the party's platform called the war a failure. This split in the Democratic Party helped Lincoln gain more support, especially from Union soldiers who wanted to see the war through to the end.

In September, things started looking up for Lincoln when General Sherman captured Atlanta, and Admiral Farragut took control of Mobile. These victories boosted morale and showed that the Union was making progress.

Finally, on November 8, 1864, Lincoln won a decisive victory in the election. He carried almost all the states except for three, and an overwhelming 78 percent of Union soldiers voted for him.

On March 4, 1865, during his second inauguration, Lincoln gave a speech that became famous. He spoke about the terrible cost of the war and hoped for peace. Lincoln said that even if the war continued until all the pain caused by slavery was paid back, it would be worth it to make things right. He called for unity and healing, asking the nation to work together for a just and lasting peace.

Lincoln's re-election showed that the people wanted him to lead the country through the rest of the war and beyond, bringing the nation together to heal its wounds and move forward as one.

Winning the Civil War

During the Civil War, President Abraham Lincoln saw General Ulysses S. Grant as a vital leader for the Union. Grant's victories at battles like Shiloh and Vicksburg impressed Lincoln. Even when others criticized Grant after Shiloh, Lincoln said, "I can't spare this man. He fights."

Lincoln believed that Grant's leadership was key to advancing the Union's cause on many fronts, including using black soldiers in the Union Army. After General George Meade didn't defeat General Robert E. Lee decisively at Gettysburg, Lincoln promoted

Grant to supreme commander, taking over Meade's army.

Lincoln was worried that Grant might want to run for president in 1864. He made sure Grant was focused on the military, not politics. Once he was sure Grant had no political plans, Lincoln promoted him to Lieutenant General—the first since George Washington. The Senate agreed on March 2, 1864.

In 1864, Grant led the Overland Campaign, a series of battles that were tough on both sides. When Lincoln asked Grant what his plans were, Grant said, "I'll keep fighting here all summer if I have to." Lincoln even visited Grant at City Point, Virginia, to talk strategy with him and other generals.

Lincoln worked hard to rally support for the Union across the North, especially after tough battles. He let Grant target Southern resources like plantations and railroads to weaken Confederate morale and strength. Lincoln wanted to defeat Confederate armies, not just destroy things.

Once, when Confederate General Jubal Early attacked Washington, D.C., Lincoln watched from the open. Legend says a Union captain told him to get down to safety, but we're not sure if that's true.

As Grant pushed Lee's forces, talk of peace started. Confederate Vice President Alexander Stephens met Lincoln and Secretary of State William Seward, but Lincoln refused to negotiate as equals. Then, on April 1, 1865, Grant almost surrounded Petersburg, and Richmond was evacuated. Lincoln visited the captured city.

Finally, on April 9, 1865, Lee surrendered to Grant at Appomattox, ending the war. Lincoln's leadership and decisions played a big part in the Union's victory.

The Tragic End of a President

Abraham Lincoln, the beloved President of the United States during a time of great turmoil, met a tragic and unexpected end. It happened one evening in April 1865, just after the Civil War had come to a close.

President Lincoln and his wife, Mary Todd Lincoln, decided to attend a play at Ford's Theatre in Washington, D.C. It was meant to be a night of relaxation and enjoyment after years of leading the country through war. As they sat in a private box watching the play, a man named John Wilkes Booth, a Confederate sympathizer and actor, quietly made his way to where the President was seated.

Booth, filled with anger and hate, approached Lincoln from behind and, without warning, fired a gunshot. The bullet struck President Lincoln in the back of his head, causing a severe and fatal injury. Major Henry Rathbone, who was with the Lincolns in the theater box, tried to stop Booth but was also injured in the struggle.

Booth managed to escape, leaving chaos and sorrow behind. President Lincoln was rushed across the street to a nearby house, but despite the efforts of doctors, he never regained consciousness. Abraham Lincoln passed away in the early morning hours of April 15, 1865.

The entire nation was shocked and deeply saddened by the loss of their President. Abraham Lincoln had been a symbol of hope and unity during the Civil War, and his death was a devastating blow. He was a man who had worked tirelessly to end slavery and preserve the Union.

In the days that followed, John Wilkes Booth was hunted down and eventually found. Refusing to surrender, Booth was shot by Union soldiers and died from his injuries.

Abraham Lincoln's funeral was a somber and solemn occasion. His body was laid in state in both the White House and the Capitol Rotunda, where people from all walks of life came to pay their respects. The nation mourned the loss of a great leader.

Although Abraham Lincoln's life was cut short, his legacy lives on. He is remembered as one of America's greatest Presidents, a man who fought for justice and equality for all people. His words and deeds continue to inspire us to this day.

Legacy

Abraham Lincoln's impact on American values and history is immense. Let's dive into what made him such an important figure.

Values of Freedom and Equality

Abraham Lincoln deeply believed in the values of freedom and equality for all people. He often discussed the Declaration of Independence, which states that everyone should be free and equal. Lincoln thought this was the most important idea for America.

During the Civil War, Lincoln made sure the country stayed together. He said that the United States was like a big family, and no one should leave. He wanted to make sure that everyone in every state felt like they were part of the same country.

Reuniting the Country

When Lincoln became president, some states wanted to leave the United States. Lincoln thought that was like breaking the rules of our country. He wanted to bring all the states back together and make sure everyone felt like they belonged.

After the Civil War ended, the United States became one country again. People started saying "the United States" instead of "these United States." Lincoln's work helped make our country stronger and more united.

How People Remember Lincoln

People have remembered Abraham Lincoln in different ways over time. Many people think he was one of our greatest presidents, like George Washington and Franklin Delano Roosevelt. Some people even say he was the best president ever!

Lincoln's story has been told in books, movies, and even in music. Many people around the world admire Lincoln for his leadership and his ideas about freedom and equality.

Lincoln's image has changed over the years. Some people have criticized him, but others still see him as a hero. Even today, many people look up to Lincoln and see him as a symbol of hope and freedom.

Abraham Lincoln's legacy lives on in the hearts of Americans and people all around the world. His ideas about freedom and unity continue to inspire us today.

Honest Abe

In the annals of American history, few figures are as universally admired for their integrity as Abraham Lincoln. Revered as "Honest Abe," this nickname encapsulates the essence of Lincoln's character and his unwavering commitment to honesty and integrity. But how did this iconic moniker come to define one of America's greatest presidents?

Abraham Lincoln's reputation for honesty and integrity began in his early years, rooted in the values instilled by his upbringing. Born into a humble frontier family in Kentucky, young Lincoln learned the importance of hard work, honesty, and fairness from his parents. His mother, Nancy, often shared stories emphasizing the importance of telling the truth and treating others with respect.

As a young man, Lincoln embarked on a journey that would shape his character and reputation. His experiences as a store clerk, rail-splitter, and self-taught lawyer further solidified his commitment to honesty in all aspects of life. Lincoln's honesty was not just a personal virtue but a guiding principle that influenced his approach to law, politics, and leadership.

One of the most famous anecdotes illustrating Lincoln's honesty dates back to his early career as a store clerk in New Salem, Illinois. Legend has it that he once realized he had shortchanged a customer by a few cents. Despite the error being in his favor, Lincoln closed the store and walked for miles to deliver the correct change to the customer, demonstrating his integrity even in a minor transaction.

Lincoln's reputation for honesty became widely known as he entered the legal and political arenas. As a lawyer, his straightforward and ethical approach earned him the trust of clients and colleagues alike. His honesty and fairness in handling legal disputes earned him the respect of his peers and adversaries.

The nickname "Honest Abe" gained prominence during Lincoln's political career. As he rose through the ranks of Illinois politics and later became President of the United States, his reputation for integrity and truthfulness continued to precede him. In an era marked by political turmoil and ethical challenges, Lincoln stood out as a beacon of honesty and moral clarity.

During his presidency, Lincoln's commitment to honesty was put to the test amid the tumult of the Civil War. He faced intense pressure and criticism but remained steadfast in upholding his principles. His unwavering honesty and integrity provided a source of strength and inspiration to the nation during its darkest hours.

After his tragic assassination in 1865, Abraham Lincoln's legacy as "Honest Abe" endured. His integrity became a cornerstone of American folklore, celebrated in countless stories and anecdotes passed down through generations. Today, the nickname "Honest Abe" remains synonymous with moral courage, ethical leadership, and the enduring power of honesty in shaping history.

Champion of Freedom

Abraham Lincoln's impact on civil rights was profound, shaping the course of American history and paving the way for equality and freedom. As the 16th President of the United States during a tumultuous period, Lincoln took bold steps to end slavery and promote civil rights for all Americans.

Lincoln firmly believed that every person deserved to be free and treated equally under the law. His journey toward championing civil rights began with the Emancipation Proclamation, a historic document issued on January 1, 1863. This proclamation declared that all slaves in

Confederate states were to be set free, marking a crucial turning point in the fight against slavery.

The Emancipation Proclamation not only freed enslaved individuals but also allowed black men to join the Union army and fight for their freedom. Lincoln understood the importance of African American soldiers in the war effort and encouraged their enlistment, believing that their bravery and dedication would help end the rebellion.

Beyond the Emancipation Proclamation, Lincoln worked tirelessly to ensure that freedom and equality prevailed throughout the nation. He supported efforts to pass the Thirteenth Amendment to the Constitution, which abolished slavery in all states, forever ending the institution that had divided the country for so long.

Lincoln's commitment to civil rights was also evident in his vision for Reconstruction after the Civil War. He sought to reunite the nation and promote healing by extending forgiveness and opportunities to former Confederate states. Lincoln believed in a future where all Americans, regardless of race or background, could participate in rebuilding the nation and enjoying the benefits of freedom.

Tragically, Lincoln's life was cut short by an assassin's bullet in April 1865, just as the Civil War was coming to an end. Despite his untimely death, Lincoln's legacy as a champion of civil rights endured. His courage, compassion, and unwavering dedication to freedom laid the groundwork for the ongoing struggle for equality in America.

Navigating Native American Relations

Long before Abraham Lincoln was born, his family had experienced tragic encounters with Native Americans. His grandfather was killed by Native Americans in front of his own sons, including Lincoln's father, Thomas. When Lincoln himself served in the state militia during the Black Hawk War, he didn't see any combat.

During Lincoln's presidency, the relationship with Native Americans became even more complicated. His administration faced challenges protecting Western settlers, railroads, and telegraphs from Indian attacks.

In August 1862, a conflict known as the Dakota War erupted in Minnesota. This conflict was extremely devastating, resulting in the deaths of hundreds of settlers and the displacement of thousands from their homes. The situation alarmed Washington deeply, with some fearing it might be part of a Confederate conspiracy.

President Lincoln took swift action. He ordered thousands of Confederate prisoners of war to be sent by railroad to help quell the uprising. However, when Confederates protested against this policy, Lincoln revoked it, ensuring that no Confederate prisoners were sent to Minnesota.

To manage the crisis, Lincoln appointed General John Pope as the commander of the new Department of the Northwest. During this time, Native American tribes like the Fond Du Lac band of Chippewa expressed a desire to fight alongside the United States against the Sioux, proposing to use their own rules of warfare, which involved no prisoners, surrender, or peace agreements.

Despite these offers, Lincoln did not accept them because he could not control the Chippewa's methods, which included the targeting of women and children in warfare.

Congressman Henry H. Sibley, serving under General Pope, played a crucial role in leading U.S. forces against the Native American forces. Sibley eventually defeated Little Crow's forces at the Battle of Wood Lake.

After the war, Lincoln faced the challenging task of deciding the fate of those captured and accused of war crimes. A military commission reviewed their actions, and Lincoln personally examined the trial transcripts. He showed compassion by commuting the sentences of many while others were executed.

Lincoln's actions during this time reflected his commitment to justice and the complexities of managing conflicts during a turbulent period in American history.

Mary's Support

In the bustling city of Springfield, Illinois, Abraham Lincoln often found solace in the company of his wife, Mary. They were a team—Abraham with his tall stature and thoughtful gaze and Mary with her sharp intellect and elegant manner. Together, they faced the challenges of life with unwavering support for each other.

Abraham admired Mary's keen mind and sought her counsel on matters of great importance. In their modest home, over candlelit dinners, they would discuss the state of the nation and the pressing issues of the day. Mary's insights were not just valued; they were indispensable to Abraham, who respected her opinions and cherished her wisdom.

As Abraham's political career took off, Mary stood by his side, attending rallies and social gatherings. Her presence brought warmth and vitality to the events, and Abraham often credited Mary with helping him connect with people from all walks of life.

During the trying years of the Civil War, Abraham bore the weight of a divided nation on his shoulders. It was Mary's unwavering support that anchored him through the storm. When doubts crept into Abraham's mind, Mary was there to reassure him with her unwavering belief in his leadership.

Amidst the chaos of war and the challenges of the presidency, Abraham and Mary found solace in their shared love and companionship. Mary's strength and resilience inspired Abraham to persevere, even in the face of adversity.

Together, they weathered personal tragedies—the loss of their young son, Willie, and the strain of war that weighed heavily on their hearts. Yet, through it all, they remained a formidable team, facing life's trials with courage and determination.

Abraham Lincoln's legacy is not just one of political leadership but also of a partnership built on love and mutual respect. Mary's unwavering support and companionship were essential to Abraham's success and enduring impact on American history.

Tad and Willie in the White House

In the bustling White House, amid the weight of the Civil War, Abraham Lincoln found solace in the joy of his sons, Tad and Willie.

Thomas Lincoln, nicknamed "Tad" by his father as a short form of "tadpole" because he was a squirmy, hyperactive child, was the youngest of three Lincoln boys. He suffered from a cleft palate, which caused him speech problems. Despite his challenges, Tad's lively spirit and mischievous antics brought laughter and warmth to the White House.

Tad had a pet goat named Nanny that he loved to play with in the White House halls, much to the chagrin of the staff. He was known for his playful antics and was always looking for adventure.

Willie, the older brother, was more reserved but deeply caring. He had a keen interest in the arts and enjoyed drawing and playing the violin. Willie often took on a protective role over Tad, looking out for his younger brother with a kind heart.

Together, Tad and Willie brought laughter and warmth to the White House during a tumultuous time. They would often explore the grounds and even sneak into their father's office, where they would climb on his lap and listen to his stories. Lincoln cherished these moments with his boys, finding respite from the weighty matters of the nation.

Tragically, Willie fell ill with typhoid fever in 1862, devastating the family. Abraham and Mary Lincoln were heartbroken, and Tad was deeply affected by the loss of his beloved brother. The White House was filled with grief, and Lincoln mourned deeply for Willie, who was only 11 years old.

Despite their sorrow, Tad and Abraham Lincoln remained close. Tad continued to bring joy to the White House with his playful nature and love for adventure. He was a reminder of youthful spirit amid somber times.

The bond between Abraham Lincoln and his sons, especially Tad and Willie, reflects the human side of a president who carried the weight of a nation on his shoulders.

A Thanksgiving Tale

In the heart of the White House during the tumultuous years of the Civil War, President Abraham Lincoln faced many challenges. But amidst the weighty matters of state, there was a lighthearted and heartwarming story that unfolded one Christmas season.

It all began when a live turkey arrived at the White House, destined for the Lincoln family's holiday feast. Like many others before it, this turkey was meant to be enjoyed as part of a festive meal. However, when President Lincoln's youngest son, Tad, laid eyes on the turkey, a different idea took hold.

Tad was just a boy, full of curiosity and compassion. He had a special affinity for animals and couldn't bear the thought of this turkey meeting its fate on the dinner table. Moved by his son's earnest plea, President Lincoln decided to humor Tad's request.

"Jack," Tad named the turkey, and he soon became a beloved companion around the White House grounds. Tad and Jack were inseparable, with Tad teaching the turkey tricks and treating him like a pet rather than a future meal.

As Christmas drew near, President Lincoln faced a dilemma. He needed to explain to Tad that Jack was intended for their holiday dinner. However, seeing the bond between Tad and Jack, President Lincoln couldn't break his son's heart.

On Christmas Eve, President Lincoln made a decision. He presented Tad with a special card—a presidential pardon for Jack the turkey. This act of kindness spared Jack's life and ensured that he would live out his days in peace.

This simple act of compassion by President Lincoln, inspired by his son's empathy, became a heartwarming tradition. It showed that even in the midst of great challenges, kindness and compassion could prevail.

MARK LYLANI

CONCLUSION

As we conclude our journey through the life of Abraham Lincoln, we reflect on the enduring legacy of a remarkable leader who faced adversity with courage and conviction. From his humble beginnings in a log cabin to the highest office in the land, Lincoln's story teaches us valuable lessons about resilience, compassion, and the power of determination.

Abraham Lincoln's impact on history cannot be overstated. He led the nation through one of its darkest periods, navigating the Civil War with steadfast resolve and a vision for unity. His Emancipation Proclamation transformed the course of American history, paving the way for freedom and equality.

Throughout his life, Lincoln embodied the principles of honesty, integrity, and empathy. His commitment to justice and equality continues to inspire generations around the world. As we look back on Lincoln's legacy, let us carry forward his spirit of perseverance and hope, striving to create a better world for all.

In honoring Abraham Lincoln's memory, we celebrate the enduring values that define us as a nation: freedom, equality, and the pursuit of a more perfect union. Let us draw inspiration from his example and work together to build a future where all individuals are treated with dignity and respect.

Thank you for joining us on this incredible journey through the life of Abraham Lincoln. May his legacy continue to shine as a beacon of hope and unity for generations to come.

Printed in Great Britain
by Amazon

58371621R00079